PECULIAR PETS

Words Of Wonder

Edited By Allie Jones

First published in Great Britain in 2021 by:

YoungWriters® Est. 1991

Young Writers
Remus House
Coltsfoot Drive
Peterborough
PE2 9BF
Telephone: 01733 890066
Website: www.youngwriters.co.uk

All Rights Reserved
Book Design by Ashley Janson
© Copyright Contributors 2020
Softback ISBN 978-1-80015-247-2

Printed and bound in the UK by BookPrintingUK
Website: www.bookprintinguk.com
YB0460E

★ FOREWORD ★

Welcome Reader!

Are you ready to discover weird and wonderful creatures that you'd never even dreamed of?

For Young Writers' latest competition we asked primary school pupils to create a Peculiar Pet of their own invention, and then write a poem about it! They rose to the challenge magnificently and the result is this fantastic collection full of creepy critters and amazing animals!

Here at Young Writers our aim is to encourage creativity in children and to inspire a love of the written word, so it's great to get such an amazing response, with some absolutely fantastic poems. Not only have these young authors created imaginative and inventive animals, they've also crafted wonderful poems to showcase their creations and their writing ability. These poems are brimming with inspiration. The slimiest slitherers, the creepiest crawlers and furriest friends are all brought to life in these pages – you can decide for yourself which ones you'd like as a pet!

I'd like to congratulate all the young authors in this anthology, I hope this inspires them to continue with their creative writing.

★ CONTENTS ★

Calcot Junior School, Calcot

Khadeja Shadoobuccus (8)	1
Danny Broadhurst (7)	2
Grace Philogene (9)	4
Olivia Heney (9)	6
Grace Turnbull (9)	7
Cody Aaron Halls (7)	8
Tristan Piper (8)	9
Kacie Rooney (7)	10
Lewie Brown (8)	11
Conor Zuccaro (8)	12
Daniel Myrdal (7)	13
Evie Lloyd (8)	14
Nailah Bouaroua (8)	15
Charlie Howard	16
Max Settle (8)	17
Joseph Whiteland (8)	18
Rory Russ (8)	19
Abaan Hussain (8)	20
Kiran Bhoot (8)	21
Harry Farrant Clark (7)	22
Jake Perrow	23
Layla Southern	24
Zak Theys	25
Aria Sissons (8)	26
Miley Turner	27
Lucas Fairchild (8)	28
Ava Alleyne	29
Leona Koroma	30
Toby Mann (8)	31
Mikey Wilson (7)	32
Katelynn Moodley (8)	33
Bruce Fashola (7)	34
Charlie Clifford (8)	35
Raymond Giles	36
Scarlett Tipper	37
Ava Duly (9)	38
Issac Layhe (8)	39
Daisy Barker	40
Gabriel Carvalho de Medeiros	41
Annabelle Truran (7)	42
Hugo Boshier (8)	43
Megan Bennellick	44
Dua Faisal (8)	45
Micky Doyle (7)	46
Lewis Sayer (8)	47
Harry Jones (7)	48
Avin Haider	49
Olivia Tidswell (7)	50
Amelia Hazelton (8)	51
Hesali Gamage (7)	52

St Anthony's Primary School, Spateston

Sinead Smith (10)	53
Eilidh Fitzpatrick (9)	54
Ella Whitehorn (10)	55
Curtis Moore (10)	56
Max Macdonald (10)	57
Ciara Orr (10)	58
Lucy Tonge	59
Poppy	60

St Mary's Hare Park School, Gidea Park

Grace Abbey (10)	61
Pearle Peacock (8)	62
Esme Pham (7)	63
Mia Macween (9)	64

Mia Joseph (9)	65
Jimi Mgbatogu (9)	66
Alessio Ahilan (8)	67
Lia Joseph (9)	68

St Monica's Primary School, Cathays

Massimo Martina (9)	69
Ariella Ademu (10)	70
Ayesha Pande (10)	72
Lisa Green (9)	73
Suhana Moktan (9)	74
Parveen Aslan (10)	76
Ffion Whittington (9)	77
Avin Momennasab (9)	78
Solomon Odiase (9)	80
Seren Burrows McDuff (10)	81
Emmanuel Ikwueto (8)	82
Mohamed Seedahmed (10)	83
Esme McAlpine (8)	84
Ilhan Rahman (8)	85
Owen Bowers (9)	86
Ajwa Syed (9)	87
David Nmesomachukwu Joseph (8)	88
Jil Anyaike (9)	89
Greatness Presley-Okpogor (9)	90
Eliot Taylor (8)	91
Constance Van Rijn (8)	92
Goodness Presley-Okpogor (8)	93
Alonso Torres (9)	94
Brenda Iheakaram (10)	95
Phoevos Diolatzis (10)	96
Brendan Iheakaram (10)	97
Hammad Sultan (9)	98
Valerie Ademu (8)	99
Nathaniel James (9)	100
David Odiase (8)	101

St Thomas Cantilupe CE Primary, Hereford

Bethan Morgan (9)	102
Mila Tomev (9)	103
Liam Fletcher (9)	104
Megan Barnett (10)	105
Andrei Gavrilas (10)	106
Cody Price (10)	107
Ava Williams (10)	108
Lilly-Mae Hobson (11)	109
Lena Karczewska (10)	110
Julia Koleczek (8)	111
Phoebe Parry (9)	112
Cobie Jackson (7)	113
Kezia Pritchard (10)	114
Betty Byng (10)	115
Fabian Rucki (8)	116
Muhammad Ismael (10)	117
Anamar Pires (10)	118
Sam Jones (11)	119
Lily Fletcher (7)	120
Alarna Lloyd (7)	121
Theo Simner (9)	122
Bruno Janusz (7)	123
Maria Tomev (7)	124
Bella Hall (7)	125
Olivia Racis (7)	126
Riley Powell (7)	127
Tommy Gargan (7)	128
Jaya Shellam (8)	129
Alan Podgorski (7)	130
Rio Whittingham (8)	131
Ted Waters (7)	132
Alejandro Roibu (7)	133
Tyson Harris	134
Gina Tangjaritsakul (7)	135
Marcel Kozaczynski (8)	136

Stanford Junior School, Brighton

Abe Garner (8)	137
Mia Maclean (10)	138

The Literacy House International, Tintagel

Emir Bayar (9)	139
Nolan Noronha (11)	140
Tahir Eralp Guzel (9)	143
Layan Alachkar (8)	145
Hani Alachkar (11)	147

Ullapool Primary School, Ullapool

Perla Nutu (8)	149
Isabella Macdonald (8)	150
Lily Maclean (10)	151
Rhea Macleod (7)	152
Lily Walton (9)	153
Ewan Ross (8)	154
Scarlett Davis (8)	155
Chloe Hodgkinson (7)	156
James Miller (9)	157
Brodie Mackenzie (9)	158
Alisha Haughey (8)	159
Lucas Mackay (9)	160

Warwick Bridge Primary School, Warwick Bridge

Joseph Powley (9)	161
Oliver Kelly (10)	162
Noah Samuel Fielden (9)	163
Harry James Richardson (8)	164
Elena Lily Archibald (9)	165
Eliza Forster (9)	166
Charlie Broatch (9)	167
Colin Abbott (9)	168
Oliver Horne (9)	169
Olivia Brown (9)	170
Will James Mackie (8)	171
Georgia Fricker (8)	172
Ava-Mae Wilson-Marks (9)	173
Jasmine Loader (8)	174
Elsa Watson (8)	175
Dylan Mackay (10)	176

West Primary School, Paisley

Finlay James Kerr (7)	177
Logan Deery Bruce	178
Sarah Garrett (7)	179
Abyaan Memon (8)	180

Westminster Community Primary School, Ellesmere Port

Imogen Turner (8)	181
Sean Machell (7)	182
Summer Forde (7)	183
Jayden Cato (7)	184

THE POEMS

Rabbity Ribbity

R abbity Ribbity is cute and tall,
A s tall as a gate and as round as a ball.
B right and colourful with splodges of green fur.
B ut she is too shy to show you a clever trick.
I n the wind blows her rusty-coloured floppy ears.
T an and white fur all over her back.
Y ou know when she is happy when her black eyes glitter.

R unning and hopping around the garden with my fluffy slipper.
I n the sun we explore nature,
B urrowing through the deep underground, she is not afraid of danger.
B edtime comes and her fur turns to gleaming gold.
I hold her tight as we each whisper stories in the night.
T ucked up in my arms, keeping each other warm when it's cold.
Y ou have to watch her when she wakes up as she's ready for another adventure!

Khadeja Shadoobuccus (8)
Calcot Junior School, Calcot

Bossy Bill Can't Sit Still

He is grumpy; he's crazy and has gigantic eyes.
No one can trust him though he tells lots of lies.
He's slimy and colourful and very very lazy.
He always jumps around and drives everyone crazy.

Bossy Bill is dangerous but very clever too.
He likes to scare people by always shouting boo!
He runs and runs around but he never stops.
He even knocks things over when he runs around in shops.

He knocks at people's doors and then he runs away.
He does this to annoy the neighbours and does it day to day.
When they say, "Bossy Bill was that you at my door?"
He lies to them and says, "Not me but I'm also not too sure."

Bossy Bill lied and said he saw a big drone.
When in fact all he saw was his neighbours dog's bone.
He said, "Look there's a huge blue worm riding on the bus."
Everyone looked to see what was the fuss.

Bossy Bill laughed and jumped and he ran.
He shouted back, "You can't catch me, catch me if you can."
Bossy Bill ran and then fell down the drain.
And crazy Bossy Bill was never seen again.

Danny Broadhurst (7)
Calcot Junior School, Calcot

My Magical Pet

My love my cute little pet
I love her but she tends to get wet!
Oh her cute little soft tail
I clearly remember when we met a whale
Her horn is so lovely and blue
If you met her you'd say, "I love you too"
Her skin is as soft as silk
And her favourite drink, well it's milk
Oh her playful heart
And her love for sweet apple tart
One day I took her for a walk
I discovered she could talk
Not like humans but a different way
And she walks in a sort of sway
She loves to play and cheer
And jumps up when friends come near
What she daily eats
Is milk and special homemade treats
When it's winter and there is snow
She seems to say to the snowflakes "Hello"

When we visit the great jungle and trees
She is so excited and she wants cheese.

Grace Philogene (9)
Calcot Junior School, Calcot

Dog Power

Dogs, cats, mice, rats they are all part of our life as we live.
I want a dog as much as can be
They just are a big success to the world
I love them with all of my heart.
The wagging of their tails as people walk by,
Just liking them and barking 'Hi'
They are friendly little creatures throughout their life
They're such loving animals here and there
They can sense when you're feeling worried or scared,
They lick you on the face and you give them a hug,
Your problems are safe with them, the cute dog.
Without a dog your life is a little bit more empty
On those days when you lose your confidence,
your best friend 'dog' can bring it back
Just with a lick or a tail wag.

Olivia Heney (9)
Calcot Junior School, Calcot

Hubber Bubba

H ubber Bubba is an incredible pet to have, she is sassy like me.
U nique, there is no other bunny like her.
B unnies are the best pets to have like Hubber Bubba.
B ubba is her nickname.
E veryone wants to be her friend, that's why she has so many wild friends.
R acing through the fields with her best friends, oh what fun she has.

B ubba enjoys some juicy carrots and cherries.
U nlike the other bunnies she is very cuddly.
B efore her bedtime I read her a story while stroking her snow-white fur.
B eautifully she lies in bed.
A sleep dozing she is snoring like you wouldn't believe.

Grace Turnbull (9)
Calcot Junior School, Calcot

Jake The Flying Hedgehog

There once was a flying hedgehog called Jake
Whom lived in the forest and liked eating cake
He spent most of his day having a great holiday
He flew to Rome
Then couldn't get home
So he followed a plane
And ended up in Spain

I held onto Jake's legs the whole time
Then I started to write this rhyme
My arms became tired
I hoped I was not fired
By my pet Jake the hedgehog

As Jake loves to eat cake
We went home to bake
A lovely cream pie and ate

Then we sat and looked at photos
Of our great adventure hocus pocus
And awoke to find out it was a dream
What a wonderful dream to awake from.

Cody Aaron Halls (7)
Calcot Junior School, Calcot

Super Molecat To The Underground Rescue!

S uper Molecat to the rescue
U nderground villains aren't a problem for Super Molecat
P urrfect ways to stop the villain
E arth soil is never hard to get through for Super Molecat
R ummage through the soil to get to the bad guys

M r Mean Mole is his worst enemy
O ver the train track is Mr Mean Mole's hideout
L ook! Mr Mean is slowing the train down
E ek Super Molecat is here
C an Super Molecat save the day
A ct fast before he captures the people
T hen Super Molecat gets a rope lasso and pulls the train away from Mr Mean.

Tristan Piper (8)
Calcot Junior School, Calcot

Rosie The Rabbit

Rosie is the most beautiful cute rabbit ever seen,
You will never guess where she has been.
She hopped to the moon
And said, "I will be back soon."
Rosie met a space bunny called Honey who had lots of money.
They are both very funny.
Rosie has red roses growing out of her fur, tiny claws with big paws.
Peach-coloured ears
She's as cute as deers.
Her tail is a big ball of fluff,
Honey pulled it and Rosie said, "That's enough."
She hopped back home before her mum moaned.
She went to sleep in her hutch.
The busy day had been too much.

Kacie Rooney (7)
Calcot Junior School, Calcot

Tina The Hyena

Tina the hyena is very, very funny
She's always telling jokes that make her laugh from her tummy.

Everywhere she goes she chuckles all the way
You can always hear her coming but so do her prey.

So she may be dangerous, ferocious and wild
But as a predator, I'm afraid she's rather quite mild.

When they hear her laughing they always run fast
"Ha, she'll never catch us, we always hear her laugh!"

So as you can see I have a very peculiar pet
She's the funniest, most extraordinary hyena I've ever met!

Lewie Brown (8)
Calcot Junior School, Calcot

Bernie's Adventure

Bernie was spinning faster and faster in his bright green wheel!
I opened the cage door, Bernie started to slow down.
He slowly and cautiously walked to me.
In my hand was a round, plastic ball. The ball was shiny and colourful!

I carefully placed Bernie into the ball, and he was off!
Bernie crashed into the walls
Bernie slammed into the chairs
Bernie bumped into the cupboards
He was having lots of fun!

Bernie's little legs were starting to slow down,
The ball wasn't rolling as fast.
It was time for Bernie's adventure to end.

Conor Zuccaro (8)
Calcot Junior School, Calcot

Rory The Reckless Rhino

Rory the Reckless rhino was my peculiar pet
and he had the biggest horn you have ever met.
He liked to ride around on his bike at a very fast speed
He wasn't looking where he was going and
knocked the poor old mouse in the weeds.
Rory the rhino was riding on a skateboard and
feeling really cool
He went too high and touched the sky then
splashed into a pool.
He was so heavy that he made a great big wave
And sent a crawling spider to his damp and wet grave.
Although he may be silly he is still my friend
I think he'll be reckless until the very end.

Daniel Myrdal (7)
Calcot Junior School, Calcot

NiNi The Sausage Dog

NiNi the sausage dog has magic powers
One of them is to grow her favourite flowers.

She loves a big red rose
But I hope they smell better than her smelly little toes.

NiNi the sausage dog can fly in the deep blue sky
But she can be worried if she goes a little too high.

Her main mission is to save the world
And make sure the bad guys get hurled.

She has the longest body and the shortest legs
So she isn't round and tubby like an egg.

NiNi the sausage dog is the best pet ever
Because she is exceptionally clever.

Evie Lloyd (8)
Calcot Junior School, Calcot

My Pet Nelly

Do you want to see my pet inside my house
It has whiskers like a mouse
Also it has ears just like a fluffy, soft dog
And it hops like a green frog
It's as tall as a giraffe which is tall indeed
It eats seaweed!
It has an enormous belly that you wouldn't
see on the telly
Its collar says Nelly
And it's black and white like a cow
He looks strange and I don't know how
He is not like pets you see in books
But he is kind and cuddly and I don't care how he
looks
Because he is my little Nelly.

Nailah Bouaroua (8)
Calcot Junior School, Calcot

Lazy Daisy

My name's Charlie and I have a cat named Daisy
She is super cute but very, very lazy
She lies about in her bed all day
But when we try to stroke her she runs away.

She's scared of her own shadow you see
She's scared of you and scared of me
Daisy will only come if you offer her treats
She likes her biscuits and likes her meats.

Daisy really likes to eat roast chicken
When she's finished eating she goes off licking
When her twin brother Archie goes out to play
She gets in her bed and sleeps until the next day!

Charlie Howard
Calcot Junior School, Calcot

My Gymnastic Giraffe

My gymnastic giraffe can bend herself in half,
I call her Wendy because she is so bendy.

She is better than a dog, cat or bunny
Because she is so funny.

In fact she is so flexible I can fit her in a box,
But she does sometimes chew my socks.

She has very long legs,
And for breakfast she likes eggs.

She has brilliant balance,
It is her best talent.

Her favourite move is a dangerous double backflip,
And she uses her neck to skip.

I think she is so fantastic because she is gymnastic!

Max Settle (8)
Calcot Junior School, Calcot

Coco The Super Cat

My cat is a super cat,
She wears a cape and a hat.
She flies around and saves the day.
Coco the super cat.

My cat is a super cat,
She eats cake and throws books at
Her enemy, the crocodile called Bray.
Coco the super cat.

My cat is a super cat,
She has a friend that is a bat.
Together they save the world from Bray.
Coco the super cat.

My cat is the super cat,
She comes home and we have a chat.
She sleeps on the chair, and there she stays,
I love Coco, my super cat!

Joseph Whiteland (8)
Calcot Junior School, Calcot

My Pet Snake Slinky

Some snakes are small, some snakes are long,
Some snakes get so big and become super strong.

Some snakes eat mice and some eat tasty rats,
I don't think they would like a dinner of infested bats.

People can be scared of snakes because of their size,
They are scared that they could be eaten alive.

Snakes lock their jaw to eat the prey,
Snakes will hunt for food throughout the night and day.

I have a snake called Jim, who I like to hold,
Him like all snakes their blood runs cold.

Rory Russ (8)
Calcot Junior School, Calcot

Super Budgie

My name is Super Budgie
I am in a cage, but love to sit in a tree

I am a superhero stopping people from crime
Though I am squeaky, fun-loving and smell like lime

Some people call me lazy
But I know I can be crazy

If you make a sound that creak
I will go mad and freak

Don't open the cage door
Or else I will flutter around and you will be on the floor

With my lime feathers, pointed beak and googly eyes
I am quite friendly until you poke me and turn into fries.

Abaan Hussain (8)
Calcot Junior School, Calcot

The Fantastic Mr Apple

Mr Apple is not an ordinary cat, because he flies like a bat.
He drinks lemonade, but only in the shade.
He has big brown eyes, which are great for when he flies.
Mr Apple is as gentle as a puppy, but he can be grumpy like a hungry bear.
When he runs through the rain, he finds it quite a pain.
He is very cute when he plays the flute,
but when he doesn't feel like it he gets a little trumpouneous.
When he is sad, he wishes he had a flying friend in the house.
But when he is happy, he gets very snappy.

Kiran Bhoot (8)
Calcot Junior School, Calcot

Sliemamiema In A Dangerous Place

Sliemamiema is a special lizard
Some even say is magic like a wizard.

His skin is like a colourful rainbow
But he can change it depending on his flow.

Sometimes he can turn invisible
Which I think makes him invincible.

Sliemamiema loves to eat all foods
It really depends on his mood.

He never gets to meet anyone
Because he thinks being invisible is more fun.

Sliemamiema can even survive a blizzard
I think this makes him the best kind of lizard.

Harry Farrant Clark (7)
Calcot Junior School, Calcot

Rocket Saves The World

Rocket the racoon, is off to save the world, I hope he'll be back soon.
He's flown to Mars in his spaceship to save the universe in one round trip
His spaceship is fast, with rocket jet power
His astronaut suit gives him superpowers
To fight the aliens that threaten the planet
He's so cool he never panics!
Rocket the racoon is my best friend,
When we are together the fun never ends
I love to hear about the adventures he's had
Everyone thinks that he is rad!

Jake Perrow
Calcot Junior School, Calcot

Nah Nah

N ever gives up
A lways ready
H as a big imagination

N o doubts
A dorable in any way
H ealthy no matter what.

Nah Nah is always good
Like she should
She never fails me
Always tells me
She's the best pet
I've ever met
She loves to sing loves to dance
All she does is prance and prance
So if you ever see me with this pet
It would be the best pet you've ever met.

Layla Southern
Calcot Junior School, Calcot

Catosaurous

C atosaurous is a very special pet
A t night it wants to play
T eeth as sharp as a lion, it loves meat
O n its fur it has lots of colours
S ometimes Catosaurous pounces on its prey
A nd enjoys the meal
U nder the floppy mane you can see its green eyes
R uns very quickly to get its prey
O ften found in the wild
U nder the large canopy trees
S ee if you can spot him in the jungle!

Zak Theys
Calcot Junior School, Calcot

Foffer The Laugher

I have a pet
My pet is the best

She has sparkly pink fur
Her tail has a cute curl
Curled like a pig
And she isn't big

She's small like a mouse
And she lives in my house

If you give her a tickle
And make her giggle
She's now the size of a cheetah
I hope she won't eat ya

Act fast
Make her laugh
And she shrinks back all tiny

You might prefer her like that!

Aria Sissons (8)
Calcot Junior School, Calcot

Louis The Hamster

Louis, Louis,
You're so tiny
Unlike a frog
You aren't slimy
You sit there smiling
Covered in fur
Unlike a cat
You don't purr
You have sharp teeth
Just like a shark
Unlike a dog
You don't bark
Your morning breakfast
Full of seeds
Unlike a mole
You don't eat weeds
You don't like worms
Spiders, or bugs
There's one thing you do like
Giving me hugs.

Miley Turner
Calcot Junior School, Calcot

The Rather Peculiar Pet

B uster is a rather peculiar pet who thinks he is a sheep.
U sually known as Sean with his white and fluffy fur, he goes, "Baa," in his sleep
S uccessfully lazy, on long walks he will refuse to move and just lie down
T reats are his favourite and he gets the best ones in town.
E veryone loves him because he gives the most amazing cuddles
R udely though he ignores commands and wees in muddy puddles!

Lucas Fairchild (8)
Calcot Junior School, Calcot

My Marvellous Magic Molly

I love my Marvellous Magic Molly but she is a peculiar pet
She loves to eat cheese but she hates the vet
Molly can fly really fast and high in the sky
Up, up, up she can go so very high
She is also super strong and can carry all the shopping
She can run a thousand miles without even stopping
I love Marvellous Magic Molly so much she is my very best friend
We will be friends together forever right until the end.

Ava Alleyne
Calcot Junior School, Calcot

My Favourite Pet

I have a panda who is three years old
She is called Lola.
She is black and white and very cute.
My panda likes to eat bamboo.
Lola is my special pet because she adorable,
Cheerful and always makes me happy.

I take her out for walks regularly and she likes
To play in the green grass.
Lola likes the smell
Of the green grass so she rolls herself and
Gets herself covered in grass.

Leona Koroma
Calcot Junior School, Calcot

Rocky The Racoon

Rocky is a racoon,
Was going to school soon,
Not like school for me and you,
It doesn't have tables and chairs too!

Rocky the racoon,
His school was the lagoon,
He only learns under the moon,
Catching fish and climbing rocks,
Eating mice and sometimes your old socks!

Rocky the racoon,
Plays the guitar like no other star,
Rocky the racoon,
Goes la, la, la!

Toby Mann (8)
Calcot Junior School, Calcot

The Giganta Frog

There was a giganta frog,
Sitting on a log,
Fed up of eating flies,
He had his eyes set on a new prize.

A dog looking for a log came sniffing past,
The greedy frog had to act fast,
Delicious lunch at last!

The slippery, slimy beast,
Was extra happy about his feast,
But the dog,
Jumped off the log,
Leaving the frog, in the bog,
Chewing a clog!

Mikey Wilson (7)
Calcot Junior School, Calcot

Rainbowed The Iguana

Rainbow ball is a big fluffy rainbow iguana
She jumps high in the sky, shining for everybody to enjoy.
Changing from bright colours to dark colours.
But she only comes out when rain has fallen and the sun begins to shine.
She only lasts a few minutes, but those few minutes feel like a lifetime.
After a few minutes she jumps back down
And turns into a small grumpy slimy green iguana.

Katelynn Moodley (8)
Calcot Junior School, Calcot

Nobody Is Better Than This Cat

As quick as a cheetah, the cat flies by,
All the robbers in the house say bye,
Because the great and awesome Ramon is flying past,
The robbers forget their plan to rob very fast.

No way the cat forgets his places,
The flash is too hurtful for the robbers' faces,
I love my cat's job,
Shame the robbers can't rob!

Bruce Fashola (7)
Calcot Junior School, Calcot

Fred The Frog

I have a frog
He sits on a log
His name is Fred
He jumps on my bed
He is small but green
So can be seen
A happy frog and never mean

Fred swims in my bath
And makes me laugh
He jumps so high
He can reach the sky
He likes to eat flies
But I prefer pies
I think he is great
He is my best mate!

Charlie Clifford (8)
Calcot Junior School, Calcot

The Cool Giraffe

My giraffe is cool
He plays in the pool
He likes to eat leaves off trees
But doesn't eat the honey from the bees
He likes to play with his toy train.
His other favourite toy is his toy plane.
He likes to go for walks in the park
But definitely not in the dark.
At night Giraffe loves to rest his head
On the bed.

Raymond Giles
Calcot Junior School, Calcot

My Pet Cog

She chased the stick across the grass and shook it in her mouth when she got it.
She was pleased with herself, my pet cog.
Her name is Willow.
Acts like a dog but looks like a cat.
A small, fluffy tabby who's a little flabby.
She has a favourite teddy that she cuddles in her bed.
His name is Fred.
Willow the cog.

Scarlett Tipper
Calcot Junior School, Calcot

The Caped Cat

C at coming to the rescue
A lways on the lookout
P rowling the streets at night
E ating out of the bins and
D ancing in the moonlight with his

C olourful, bright, feathery cape
A nd he has tiger-like eyes
T hat glow against his silky black fur.

Ava Duly (9)
Calcot Junior School, Calcot

Maw Maw The Grumpy Pet

Maw Maw the moaning pet
Arguing angrily getting in a tangliy.
Waggling, wailing waves of woe when Maw Maw is away from home.
Maw Maw meows with glee using his sharp teeth to clear his fleas.
A happy chappy Maw Maw when he's back where he belongs.
Wow, wow, wow what a weird wild pet!

Issac Layhe (8)
Calcot Junior School, Calcot

Super Summer's Powers

Super Summer has black and white fur.
She has powers inside her.
She shoots ice out of her claws
And blows out fire when she snores.
She can hear from a mile away.
And she loves to play.
She whips her tail at your face.
She runs so fast you can't catch her in a race.

Daisy Barker
Calcot Junior School, Calcot

Flames The Golden Dragon

He's shiny
He breathes golden dust
He's as marvellous as a golden bar
He hatched out of a golden egg
Only to be found in the golden cave over 1 million years ago.
They've gone extinct, there's the only one in the world
And it's my Flames!

Gabriel Carvalho de Medeiros
Calcot Junior School, Calcot

Super Parrot

S uper parrot
U sually wild
P lenty of colours
E xtraordinary powers
R eally super.

P icsy,
A dorable parrot
R eally cute
R eally fast
O ften naughty
T iny parrot.

Annabelle Truran (7)
Calcot Junior School, Calcot

Spy Lawrence Spy

L icking you to pick up your scent.
A lways alert
W hite for camouflage
R uns at the speed of light
E xtraordinary
N aughty when he needs to be.
C ute because he's a llama
E lementary spy llama.

Hugo Boshier (8)
Calcot Junior School, Calcot

Tundra

T is for totally terrific
U is for unstoppable and competitive
N is for noisy and unbelievably naughty
D is for daring and dangerous
R is for radical and ruthless
A is for adventurous.

Megan Bennellick
Calcot Junior School, Calcot

Cute Panda

Grumpy but cute
Clever also tiny
Quite lazy and messy
Always adorable
Scared of spiders
Love crafter
Scared of strange noises also scared of strange things.
Makes a mess when cutting
Loves to eat bamboo.

Dua Faisal (8)
Calcot Junior School, Calcot

Jack

J umping to train hard in his training room
A lways protecting people far and near.
C lever caring Jack can fly and save people with his superpowers.
K ind and helpful gorilla is loved by everyone.

Micky Doyle (7)
Calcot Junior School, Calcot

Ruby The Racoon

Ruby the racoon is a shape-shifter and more,
She is unlike any other pet before,
She can do lots of things like no others can do,
Because she's Ruby the racoon and likes to do number twos!

Lewis Sayer (8)
Calcot Junior School, Calcot

Jason The Monkey

My monkey has fluffy fur and it feels happy.
He is cute and lazy.
He is gentle and incredible.
He is marvellous and adorable.
He loves to be messy and is extraordinary.

Harry Jones (7)
Calcot Junior School, Calcot

My Fish Nemo

I have a fish and it is called Nemo,
He loves to swim and he loves to sleep,
His favourite number is zero,
I clean his tub every week,
He loves going below the water.

Avin Haider
Calcot Junior School, Calcot

Harry The Hungry Hamster

Harry the hamster likes to eat carrot,
It would have been easier having a parrot.

He likes his tummy to be full,
Soon he will be as round as a ball!

Olivia Tidswell (7)
Calcot Junior School, Calcot

My Magic Cat

M arvellous orange eyes
A lways caring about me
G orgeous thick, soft fur
I ntelligent and amazing
C oolest cat ever!

Amelia Hazelton (8)
Calcot Junior School, Calcot

Rose The Amazing Dog

R ose loves to look at rainbows
O utside she likes to play
S he's good at dancing
E nds up eating dog biscuits.

Hesali Gamage (7)
Calcot Junior School, Calcot

Sassy Sally!

This is Sally and Sally is sassy!
Sally likes handbags and hanging out with her friends,
Sally has an attitude, maybe a lot of it...
Anyway, her room is always a mess - I always have to clean it,
She thinks, *I'm a queen*, and she prances about like one thinking she is royalty.
Sally is like a monkey though because she super funky,
But Sally is my best friend, so I will join her.
Sassy is a style now but my Sally, the sassy frog, will always be the most sassiest of all!

Sinead Smith (10)
St Anthony's Primary School, Spateston

Pamela The Purple Dancing Panda

Pamela is the best,
She is the most fabulous panda ever.
She dances everywhere
She is as beautiful as a swan.
Then suddenly *crash! Bang!*
She was turning, and she fell.
But she never gives up,
So she continued to turn round and round.
She went to her dance competition and she won!
She is so adorable and purple,
She wears a pink tutu and a pink bow.
She went to bed and she was as gentle as flowing trees.

Eilidh Fitzpatrick (9)
St Anthony's Primary School, Spateston

Harold The Hedgehog

While exploring the wood, a little creature came out.
He was a tiny hedgehog, I picked him up he was as prickly as a pinecone and off we went.
He said his name was Harold
I just laughed, haha!
I got him a little house he said he loved it,
I was happy we went everywhere together,
My sister wanted him gone I told her to go away,
We went back to wood he came from,
He found his hedgehog family and I never saw him again.

Ella Whitehorn (10)
St Anthony's Primary School, Spateston

Super Dog

S uper Dog is super strong.
U p, up, and away is where he belongs.
P elicans fly right beside him.
"E veryone, look at me, I can fly up high".
R ain is Super Dog's favourite weather.

D o not worry, Super Dog is coming to save the day!
O pen up your windows and give him a clap.
G reen is Super Dog's favourite colour.

Curtis Moore (10)
St Anthony's Primary School, Spateston

Special Vegas

Special Vegas the gentle giant.
Is 100% happy and extraordinary.
Despite his size he acts like a mouse and would never be seen chasing a grouse.
His nose is special and loves to explore yet he can't find me behind a door!
His coat is so black and shiny, but his bum is super stinky.

Max Macdonald (10)
St Anthony's Primary School, Spateston

On The Farm

Down at the farm today there is Lulu the lavender llama,
She wears rockstar glasses and causes a drama.
She runs with the sheep and ends up in a heap,
She drew a hawk with some chalk,
She throws rocks and gets caught,
At the end of the day Lulu gets lazy so she decides to smell daisies.

Ciara Orr (10)
St Anthony's Primary School, Spateston

Things To Know About Susie The Superhero Spider

S uperhero and never gives up.
U sually saves people in danger.
S ometimes grumpy which is okay.
I nspirational to all of her members.
E very day she *never gives up!*

Lucy Tonge
St Anthony's Primary School, Spateston

My Moody Monkey Zozo

Z ozo the monkey is my extraordinary pet
O pened doors I know who did it
Z ozo is scared of a banana and she is so lazy
O h no she is running away from me I only have a banana!

Poppy
St Anthony's Primary School, Spateston

My Wonderous Unicorn

Eyes like a sedate sunset waking the sun up from its bed
Mixed like the season, no being misled

Covered with living things such as roses
Just like the earth, what is beauty actually worth?

A smile like the River Nile flowing through the tough and rough
Making other people share the same upwards grin - you can never get enough

Its horn like your protector, it will guide you on your way
And never lead you astray

My wondrous unicorn, so special to me
It brings me joy and never-ending glee

Heaven sent to Earth.

Grace Abbey (10)
St Mary's Hare Park School, Gidea Park

Purppy Wings

P urppy Wings is my favourite pet
U p the garden she gallops
R ough? No she isn't
P urple she may be, but she's still a...
P uppy!
Y ap, yap, yap is all she says

W hen she's sleeping
I am quiet
N o she's not naughty
G rilled salmon is her favourite
S uper she is.

Pearle Peacock (8)
St Mary's Hare Park School, Gidea Park

My Super Pup

My super pup is colourful and bright,
My super pup always think she's right.
My super pup is cute, but when people say she's cute she goes mute.
My super pup has a special horn which is sharp like a thorn.
My super pup has special multicoloured boots that shoots colourful sparkly poops!
My super pup runs wild and free but in the end she comes running back to me!

Esme Pham (7)
St Mary's Hare Park School, Gidea Park

Sassy Sarah!

Sassy Sarah, my lazy cat
When I put her in the bath, she jumps right onto the bathroom mat!
She eats cake all day
Until it's time to play
At weekends when we're having tea
She sits there and stares at me
At the end of the day
It's time to say
She is an amazing sassy cat!

Mia Macween (9)
St Mary's Hare Park School, Gidea Park

Pixie Puppy

P ixie likes to play a lot and likes the snow
U sually she sleeps in my bedroom
P uppies are cute and fluffy but Pixie is energetic
P ixie loves to explore outside and finds interesting things
Y ou would like a puppy like her, she's adventurous.

Mia Joseph (9)
St Mary's Hare Park School, Gidea Park

Crox The Boss

I'm Crox the boss and you'll never catch me nappin'
Everywhere I go you'll always hear me rappin'!
I'm the best in the world, the best of all
I normally like to see a glittery disco ball!

Jimi Mgbatogu (9)
St Mary's Hare Park School, Gidea Park

Booty Boo

Booty Boo is good at football
He has ten footballs
He has really soft skin
Boo hasn't got any pins
He is intelligent and has a number 2 shirt
He hates skirts
Boo has a good time.

Alessio Ahilan (8)
St Mary's Hare Park School, Gidea Park

Daring Dolly

D aring feats that she cannot avoid
O nly the best at sports
L ilac is her favourite colour
L ovely, kind and sweet
Y oung and energetic.

Lia Joseph (9)
St Mary's Hare Park School, Gidea Park

Ninjaboom

Ninjaboom is as dangerous as a dinosaur
He's a naughty Ninjaboom
He loves karate
Ninjaboom is as fast as flash
He's very talented
Ninjaboom goes *zoom* all the time
Ninjaboom loves his claws
Ninjaboom wears a karate suit all the time
Ninjaboom is behind the shed often
He is braver than Dwane 'The Rock' Johnson
Ninjaboom's tail is softer than cotton wool
Ninjaboom's always out at night
Ninjaboom cracks wood all the time
Ninjaboom's idol is Karate Kid
Ninjaboom has fun every day
Ninjaboom loves what he does and loves his life.

Massimo Martina (9)
St Monica's Primary School, Cathays

Amazing Astri

Meet Astri my amazing cat
But she's not your average cat
She's zinging and fun in her colourful hat
But she *hates* getting it wet.

When night falls, and all are asleep,
She turns into a gorgeous phoenix with dazzling orange feathers ready to fly.

Whoosh!
She sets to the sky
Looking above all
When I see her high above,
She comes down and transforms Mega
Then I can ride on her feathery back.

Up we go,
Higher, higher and higher!
Till we reach Megaville
Where Megas and humans live in perfect harmony.

Bang!
We come down
Tired Astri turns to normal mode
We look around the place
And decide to go to the top of Mega mountain
I hold Astri with her fur as soft as a teddy.

We reach the mountain top
Astri looks at the sky
I see the passion in her eyes.

Bang!
We land back home
I go to bed
But clever Astri eats some delicious Dino nuggeties!

Ariella Ademu (10)
St Monica's Primary School, Cathays

Magical Morphi

Magical Morphi,
A peculiar pet!
Turns into a chef and makes my tea,
Never heard of him, I bet!

Turning into monsters and beasts,
Eating ice cream frequently!
Clumsily knocking down jars of treats,
Wham! Sometimes he's too much for even me!

Whizz! Whizz! Wham!
Transforms colour and shape.
Whether it's an elephant or ram,
We're always having a jolly jape!

I take him to school, and even the pool,
Tail as soft as a cloud.
He's my extraordinary, secret tool
Tail like a long pom-pom, but is that allowed?

Ayesha Pande (10)
St Monica's Primary School, Cathays

Amazing Furry Polly

F antastic cheerful Polly ran
U pstairs in my room
R ushing furiously outside to play
R uining the beautiful tidy leaves
Y awning tiredly from her long playtime

P olly was so fast that she won the golden cup
O ff she went to eat her lunch but sadly someone had stolen it
L ovely sad angry Polly went to look for food
L onely Polly unfortunately could not find anything
Y awning sadly rushing through the tidy leaves running upstairs and jumped in bed.

Lisa Green (9)
St Monica's Primary School, Cathays

The Mighty Unibutterfly!

The Unibutterfly is very clever,
Wings that are beautiful.
Does she lie? Never,
Her dancing is very wonderful.

Zooms like a race car,
But she makes no sound.
Goes to the bar,
Makes a pound.

Eats rainbow clouds,
Above the rainbow flying.
I am very proud,
I can see what she is eyeing.

Graceful as a ballerina,
Movement is very fancy.
Her friend is Lerina,
Her moves are dancy.

Lerina is very cute,
Friendly, tame.
Sometimes mute,
I am the same.

Suhana Moktan (9)
St Monica's Primary School, Cathays

Unisaurus

A dangerous creature, in the wild forest...
But loves to sing in a chorus! La la la.
His favourite food is meat,
When he's happy he loves to dance to the beat!
But he's usually angry, grrrr!
But he loves to be fancy! Oolala!
He gets sassy when he's bored...
When he's angry he roars!
People says he's adorable but he's really ferocious!
But he has lots of emotions!
He has small hands,
But he has bright sharp fangs!
He has chicken legs
And he likes to get in bed... Zzzzz.

Parveen Aslan (10)
St Monica's Primary School, Cathays

Meet Lulu

She lives in a cute bunny house
Lulu is sassy but tiny
She loves to tell knock-knock jokes
She has bullies but she just walks away
Lulu is a clever she loves maths
She goes in the car all the time to maths classes
Lulu is colourful
Pink, green and blue
She has lots of friends
They are colourful too
Lulu loves to hop, sing and dance
She eats carrots and drinks milk
Lulu eats so much her tummy is
Soooo massive
She is hungry all the time she
Rubs her tummy so much!

Ffion Whittington (9)
St Monica's Primary School, Cathays

Loopy Lolipop

Lolipop is very
Messy she
Has a sassy
Attitude
Can be very helpful most
Of the time
Cuteness is her main goal especially when
It comes to make-up
She's an adorable
Girl but
She's tiny
But nothing holds her back
She has many enemies
They
Call her
Loopy Lolipop
But she can
Be wild not
All the
Time
She lives in a colourful place called

Pink, Purple, Red, Yellow, Orange, Blue place holiday
But she's lonely very
Lonely.

Avin Momennasab (9)
St Monica's Primary School, Cathays

Amazing Afan

A dventurous when we play jungles
M indful when he listens to people
A nnoyed when I take his toys
Z zzz, don't disturb, he is sleeping
I mportant to feed him
N ever make him have a short temper
G reat and good as my pet

A mazing has razor-sharp claws and sometimes roars
F erocious noise
A ngered by people who are being too kind
N oisy and speedy. If you squeeze him the noise he makes is squeezy, squeezy, squeezy.

Solomon Odiase (9)
St Monica's Primary School, Cathays

Sassy Sam

Sassy Sam as loud as an earthquake,
Scratching at my bed,
Trying to steal my cake,
While pulling at my leg.

Sassy Sam jumping on my head,
Just as I wake up,
A smart small cat, wearing all my red,
Which made me quite fed up.

A small adventurous cat,
Looking up at the dark sky,
Even wearing my old hat,
Even trying to lie!

Spreading out his feathery wings,
For my hamsters to hop on,
Giving a small grin,
Just like that they're gone!

Seren Burrows McDuff (10)
St Monica's Primary School, Cathays

Drago The Dragon

Meet my pet Drago
he likes to stay in places that are really hallowed.
He likes to fly all around the castle
he also breaths fire just a little hassle.

He runs around all in a dash.
he runs into plants that get him a rash
He needs his rest all of the time
he sings in his sleep and he can rhyme.

He is always really really hungry for his food.
or he gets very grumpy and rude,

After all, he is a good little pet
but he really doesn't like getting wet

Emmanuel Ikwueto (8)
St Monica's Primary School, Cathays

Business Monkey

Business Monkey is very furry
Without his glasses his eyesight is blurry
Business Monkey has a lot of money
He is very funny
Business Monkey likes bananas
But he really hates katanas
Business Monkey is very fast
In a race he is never last
He lives in an office outside in the grass
Everything is made out of diamonds and glass
He has very big ears
Spiders are what he fears
I always ride on his back
His watch is shinier than a silver rack.

Mohamed Seedahmed (10)
St Monica's Primary School, Cathays

Hugo The Gentle Giant

Hugo the giraffe
Is having a laugh
He is watching a movie
A movie about smoothies, smoothies!

Hugo can change the colours of his spots because of his mood
He likes food, pineapple food
Hugo likes space
He likes to find out a new, new place

Gallop! Gallop! And he's off. Dust, oh no!
Cough! Cough! Here it comes... ahh ahh choo!
Gentle giant Hugo can't help his size
But he is no match to the crowd as he is hard to disguise.

Esme McAlpine (8)
St Monica's Primary School, Cathays

Lazy Lazari

L azy Lazari.
A very confident creature but can be lazy sometimes.
Z zzz goes little Lazari when she's lazy.
Y ou don't know how scary she is if you harrass her!

L azy Lazari.
A dorable as a newborn baby.
Z zzz goes Lazari sleeping.
A violent creature.
"R oar!" goes Lazari growling at her enemies.
I don't think she'll ever attack me.

Ilhan Rahman (8)
St Monica's Primary School, Cathays

Demond Frog

My Demond Frog has sharp teeth,
2 horns on the top of his head,
Loads of spots on the body,
1 eye,
A tail,
4 legs,
Can climb,
Can talk,
Can sniff,
Ferocious frog,
Dangerous Demond,
Energetic frog,
Super fast at running,
Lives under the ground
Quick as a flash
Ouch too quick
Stomps to the door
Crashes into the door
As round as a football

Meet Demond Frog!

Owen Bowers (9)
St Monica's Primary School, Cathays

Fly Myoon

The fantastic Myoon lives above the clouds
The rain is falling so loud
Fantastic Myoon flys to visit me at my house
but he is quiet as a mouse
Fantastic Myoon lies on the ground
like something he found
Fantastic Myoon's tail is colourful
like he is wonderful

Fantastic Myoon has a pointy head
like he has a red bed
Fantastic Myoon smiles
his grin is so big that it goes for miles.

Ajwa Syed (9)
St Monica's Primary School, Cathays

Electric Tiger

E xcellent Electric Tiger
L azy sometimes at hunting
E xtraordinary to other tigers
C lever
T rains to get stealthier
R ipping prey
I s
C lever at pouncing

T ipping over while training
I rreversible to never die
G rumpy at losing
E ating tiger never stops
R aged when it's *super* angry.

David Nmesomachukwu Joseph (8)
St Monica's Primary School, Cathays

A Chubby Magical Unicorn

A very gentle pet,
Cuddly and furry, I even sleep with him at night
Very cute, he will even make you say, "Aw!"
Many friends
Quite a few enemies
Plays with my toys
Growls at my shoes
Very weird sometimes
Enemies always annoy him,
Make him *angry*,
He controls it sometimes
Disappears without warning
Never in my life had a pet like this before!

Jil Anyaike (9)
St Monica's Primary School, Cathays

Leopacorn

Leopacorn likes to eat corn,
Little does she know she has a horn.
She likes to wonder,
When there's thunder.

Sometimes she humble,
But sometimes she stumbles.
She likes to be clever,
But we know she doesn't have a feather.

She's running towards the pool *splash!*
Oh no it's a *bash!*
She likes to stretch,
But she's the best.

Greatness Presley-Okpogor (9)
St Monica's Primary School, Cathays

Karate Cat

Karate Cat is very quick
But sometimes he drinks very fast, he goes hic!
Karate Cat is very clumsy
But he likes it when I rub his tumsy

Karate cat is very fast
In his audition cast...
But trips up!
But sometimes
Then at the break he spills his cup!
Bang! Splat!

Oh Karate Cat!

Eliot Taylor (8)
St Monica's Primary School, Cathays

Heather The Striped Elephant

She has big blue eyes
and likes to chase flies

she has lots of friends
and the fun never ends

she is always asked to be in photoshoots
but she is always buying boots

she wears a tiny crown
but she never frowns

she has rainbow stripes
which she never wipes

she has a fluffy tail
but never fails.

Constance Van Rijn (8)
St Monica's Primary School, Cathays

Flying Elephant

The Flying Elephant dashes into the clouds
He made a crash so loud
Into the blue sky
When he's flying he is so high
Landed on the ground then spins
Then he looks at me then grins
Then I stumble
His belly rumbles
He is so clever
He knows whatever
He is so cute
Wearing a suit
Long tail
Like a whale.

Goodness Presley-Okpogor (8)
St Monica's Primary School, Cathays

Drago Corn

D rago Corn is an adorable pet
R oaring in the dark night
A mazing at magic and flying
G ood and healthy
O ld but as cute as a kitten

C an live forever but stays as cute as a kitten
O ptimistic Drago Corn
R eally tamed and extraordinary
N ever gives up on things.

Alonso Torres (9)
St Monica's Primary School, Cathays

Bella The Turtle!

Bella the turtle was gentle,
And as fast as a cheetah.
She could even talk!
An extarordinary animal.
Gentle and agile.
Where danger came she went whoosh,
An incredible animal!
She could talk and run fast
She was as clever as me
She is the best pet ever.

Brenda Iheakaram (10)
St Monica's Primary School, Cathays

Crocospike

C rawling Crocospike.
R rrr!
O dd tail.
C limbing Crocospike.
O dd teeth.
S piky tail.
P ushing rocks.
I ncredible at crushing bones.
K rrr!
E xtraordinary noises bang!

Phoevos Diolatzis (10)
St Monica's Primary School, Cathays

Shelly

S pectacular Shelly is the best among us
H e is honest, humble and loyal
E xtraordinary as he is fast
L oves his owner more than himself
L ittle but can defeat 50 men
Y oung but is always wise.

Brendan Iheakaram (10)
St Monica's Primary School, Cathays

Speedy Jack

Speedy Jack as fast as the speed of light
He might give you a fright as he takes flight!
Speedy Jack as clever as a feather
He zooms as he makes a boom in any weather
You will not beat him ever!

Speedy Jack!

Hammad Sultan (9)
St Monica's Primary School, Cathays

Beeoncye

B eautiful Beeoncye
E xtraordinary pet
E xcellent singer
O n the stage
N ever misses a beat
C lever as Einstein
Y outhful and young
E very bee is jealous.

Valerie Ademu (8)
St Monica's Primary School, Cathays

Congor

C olourful Congor
O h wow when he makes dinner
N oisy when he is so bad
G reat when he wins trophies
O dd when he does yoga
R eally cheeky when he eats your shoes.

Nathaniel James (9)
St Monica's Primary School, Cathays

Antlogon

My Antlogon is very colourful
It is very wonderful
As kind as a flame
It always takes the blame.

My Antlogon has spiked jawed teeth
Eats a ball of meat
It's very slimy
And very tiny.

David Odiase (8)
St Monica's Primary School, Cathays

Simon The Rockstar Cat

Simon the rockstar cat is,
as happy as a dancing dog,
as noisy as a tambourine,
as excited as a rockstar cat,
as fast as a lightning bolt,
as silent as a weeping kitten,
as sad as a broken heart,
as extraordinary as an electric guitar,
as dangerous as a daredevil,
as ferocious as a man-eating shark,
as wild as a marvellous monkey,
as incredible as a silly scientist,
as lazy as a basset hound,
as grumpy as a gooey frog,
as clever as a life-saving doctor,
as adorable as a clever clogs.

Bethan Morgan (9)
St Thomas Cantilupe CE Primary, Hereford

Luna The Long Leg Dog!

Peculiar pets, peculiar pets
Come in all different shapes, colours and sizes.
My peculiar pet is Luna the long leg dog.
Luna the long leg dog is black with the longest legs you've ever seen.
Apart from that, she has bright pink fur, surrounding her legs, like a pink flower.
Luna the long leg dog needs attention every minute.
Scratch her or she will be sad.
Peculiar pets, peculiar pets
Come in all different sizes, colours and shapes
But Luna the long leg dog is the most peculiar pet I've ever seen.

Mila Tomev (9)
St Thomas Cantilupe CE Primary, Hereford

Fluffy Fhelix

I have a dog,
his name is Fhelix
he is not normal - he can fly.

We call him fluffy Fhelix,
He doesn't fly by his ears,
he can fly by shaking his fluffy fur.

I took him for a walk,
we were on the ground for a bit,
then we were flying, ferociously.

We all love fluffy Fhelix,
but he can get on our nerves,
we tell him to walk but he goes out flying.

This may be far-fetched,
but I'm being honest,
fluffy Fhelix has fur like a giant carpet and can fly.

Liam Fletcher (9)
St Thomas Cantilupe CE Primary, Hereford

Terry The Rock Tortoise

There are so many peculiar pets but the most peculiar pet is definitely mine .
Not powered by brain but powered by a crystal flame.
His flame hair burns everyone who touches.
The electric power sings
He's a devil against people who try to hurt justice
He's not a superhero but he's Terry the rock tortoise
Yes, a tiny tortoise more powerful than you.
A tiny tortoise who can move planets.
A tiny tortoise who can burn your fingers off.
A tiny tortoise that no one can beat.

Megan Barnett (10)
St Thomas Cantilupe CE Primary, Hereford

Super Simon The Slug

Simon can shrink as I wish.
With a huge, ferocious swish.
I climb on, a huge grin.
Stroking his slimy skin with my fingers, thin.
We rise up into the night sky.
People stare, starting to deny.
Me and Simon high.
Falling down wanting supper.
What does he prefer?
Simon rushes to a tree.
One, two, three!
He steps away, guilty.
Nothing there!
Oh no, let's go!
Flying high, drastic measures.
Assuring our wellbeing.
We fly away unsure.

Andrei Gavrilas (10)
St Thomas Cantilupe CE Primary, Hereford

Chef Cody

From my experiences with Chef Cody,
I can tell you he is a defensive duck,
He cooks and reads books
Then *boofs* ungrateful customers on the nose!

He will moan and groan if it isn't his 'perfect' pie which he considers is to die for,
I'd recommend to stay away when the duck is out to play.
To avoid temptation, you have to face humiliation,
And if you dare say no he will whack his pan to and fro
To end up until it ends up on your head.

Cody Price (10)
St Thomas Cantilupe CE Primary, Hereford

Susan The Sassy Snake

By the way Susan was acting, I could tell she wanted to go for a walk,
We hopped, skipped and jumped, we saw a panda so we talked.
Susan found a puddle... I shouted, "Oh no!"
I yelled oh no because snakes and water don't go.
Susan can't swim because she is too fat,
She scoffs herself with lasagne, she even ate the cat.
I grabbed her by her tail and dragged her home,
As we were going home, Susan groaned.

Ava Williams (10)
St Thomas Cantilupe CE Primary, Hereford

Sapphire The Teaching Dog

S apphire teaches celebrities how to be cool,
A fter that she rests in her doggy bed,
P addling her paws as she dreams of being a princess,
P rincess Sapphire naps in her royal bed,
H ospitality is her main priority,
I f she is given a pay rise she will be very happy,
'R uff!" she barks lazily as her students came,
E llie is her best friend.

Lilly-Mae Hobson (11)
St Thomas Cantilupe CE Primary, Hereford

Chip The Tap Dancing Penguin

Chip loves to tap dance at all times, in the evening and in the morning,
Incredible dancers join in the tap dance with Chip.
Radiant, ferocious polar bears join in now,
Chip the marvellous dancer will make you laugh like a volcano about to burst.
Unknown mysteries won't be solved without a riddle.
Surprisingly, Clever Chip knows what to do.
Just dance to his rhythm and the mystery will be solved.

Lena Karczewska (10)
St Thomas Cantilupe CE Primary, Hereford

Obedient Octo

O fficial, does not break the law
B reathes out of his eyes
E ats people
D angerous as a lion
I mpolite with no manners
E nergetic like a motorbike
N aughty
T roublesome with a broken heart

O bsessive
C heeky like a monkey
T errible at playing tentacle football, but
O nly on a Monday.

Julia Koleczek (8)
St Thomas Cantilupe CE Primary, Hereford

Beatrice The Dancing Pig

I have a peculiar pet,
Her name is Beatrice the dancing pig,
I go into the dancing room and see her grooving on the spot,
While eating from the biggest cereal box,
When I go to bed at night,
She turns up the volume and *boom!*
I go downstairs and see on the telly,
Doctor Who!
Beatrice disappears into thin air,
I think for a minute,
Is she a hero?

Phoebe Parry (9)
St Thomas Cantilupe CE Primary, Hereford

Shooty Paws

S wish with diamond armour
H ooligan that will not take the blame
O range like the fresh cold leaves
O rders other people to get arrested, not him
T he tickets cot in the world
Y ells like mad

P opular with his biggest fans
A cross the road with his lightning cap
W ashes in filthy water.

Cobie Jackson (7)
St Thomas Cantilupe CE Primary, Hereford

Florence The Flying, Talking And Cloth-Wearing Penguin

F unny and has an infectious laugh after talking,
L oving when playing with other penguins,
O riginal and can fly,
R ecommended for an Oscar award,
E njoyable for a pet,
N eurotic about their imaginary friend fading,
C ute and can put a smile on your face,
E xtraordinary at maths and putting on clothes.

Kezia Pritchard (10)
St Thomas Cantilupe CE Primary, Hereford

Clive The Clever Chameleon

I took Clive the clever chameleon for a walk.
He saw a panda, so decided to talk

Clive went on with his stroll
Next thing you know, he was dancing with a mole

He twirled, he leaped, cha cha cha-ed then did the jive
He took a dive in the pond!

Clive was wet, cold and shivering
I think our walk was done for today!

Betty Byng (10)
St Thomas Cantilupe CE Primary, Hereford

Super Angel Hamsters

Super angel hamsters have pink heads
With ears which are made out of snow
Berries which are poisonous to humans
They have four wings which are purple and mega feet
Their legs are silver and shiny and they can break anything!
Their tails are a fluffy as the fluffiest pillows in the world
They have very spiky ears.

Fabian Rucki (8)
St Thomas Cantilupe CE Primary, Hereford

Basil My Dancing Bull

Basil my lovely dancing bull
Loves nothing more than doing a twirl.
He lifts his tail and swings around
Any musical notes that sound.
He loves nothing more than Katy Perry
It always makes him feel merry.
He shifts his hooves from side and side
And twerks his enormous hairy hide.

Muhammad Ismael (10)
St Thomas Cantilupe CE Primary, Hereford

Dilly The Dinosaur Cleaner

Dilly the dinosaur works as a cleaner,
He cleans and he cleans,
Every night he goes home,
His children love him,
Every morning he buys them lots of lovely toys,
But they do not play with them,
However he is happy,
As they are clean!

Anamar Pires (10)
St Thomas Cantilupe CE Primary, Hereford

Super Speedy William The Wolf

As fast as light he will take flight,
William my super speedy wolf.
He takes off slow but boy can he go.
Flapping his wings aglow.
People stop to stare
At the bright orange flare
That rips across the sky
As William whizzes by.

Sam Jones (11)
St Thomas Cantilupe CE Primary, Hereford

Super Dream

Face like a baby panda
Flies as high as a turtle dove
Paws as small as a hamster's
Horn as log as a pole
Eyes as green as grass
Hair as colourful as crayons
Legs as soft as marshmallow
Body as fluffy as a blanket.

Lily Fletcher (7)
St Thomas Cantilupe CE Primary, Hereford

Monster Hamster

It will watch you whilst you're sleeping
Horns as pointy as a pair of scissors
Wings as red as a chilli pepper
Legs as long as a river
Can fly as fast as a cheetah
Teeth as sharp as a knife
Eats all the food at night.

Alarna Lloyd (7)
St Thomas Cantilupe CE Primary, Hereford

Ohm The Owl

O ptimistic
H igh flyer
M arvellous

T actical
H opeful
E xtraordinary

O ddly has ears like a fox
W ild acting
L illiputian.

Theo Simner (9)
St Thomas Cantilupe CE Primary, Hereford

Super Snake

It can stretch ten metres
It has ten legs
Its ears are just holes in its head
You can find him in fields
He's as fast as a car
He's as sneaky as a tiger
His eyes are as wet as water.

Bruno Janusz (7)
St Thomas Cantilupe CE Primary, Hereford

Uni Bear

Fur as brown as hot chocolate
Eyes as green as mint
Magic as powerful as a plane's engine
Horn as colourful as confetti
Its egg is purple with light pink specks
It loves the hot beaming sun.

Maria Tomev (7)
St Thomas Cantilupe CE Primary, Hereford

Pizza Pet

Ten super soft crusts, fluffy like a blanket
Eyes as red as pepperoni
Tail as tall as a school
Ears as crunchy as a rock
You'll find her in Pizza Hut
Mouth as round as the blazing sun.

Bella Hall (7)
St Thomas Cantilupe CE Primary, Hereford

Super Ivy

Eyes as green as the soft fluffy grass
Tail as red as a hot sunny beach
Legs as long as a tree
Brain as hard as a solid brick
Teeth as sharp as a pointy mountain
Hair as soft as a pillow.

Olivia Racis (7)
St Thomas Cantilupe CE Primary, Hereford

Elf Cat

Eyes as fluffy as a cat
Tail as soft as a blanket
As cool as a smart cat
You'll find him in the trees
Soaring over trees
Swishing over trees
Shooting cats out of his eyes.

Riley Powell (7)
St Thomas Cantilupe CE Primary, Hereford

Cheese Paws

Five yellow cheesy paws
Eyes as red as a fiery sunset
Feet as stinky as blue cheese
Teeth as fresh as mouth wash
Legs as long as a skyscraper
Wings as burned as crusted toast.

Tommy Gargan (7)
St Thomas Cantilupe CE Primary, Hereford

Uni Bunny

Crystal eyes like the blue sky
Red, fiery body
Paws as soft as fluff inside of a teddy bear
Unicorn horn as long as a pole
Eyelashes as wet as the dew on the grass.

Jaya Shellam (8)
St Thomas Cantilupe CE Primary, Hereford

Roar

It has four tentacles
It has colourful wings and colourful legs
Its hands are on the end of its legs
It is evil
If you look at it it will turn you into paper.

Alan Podgorski (7)
St Thomas Cantilupe CE Primary, Hereford

Silly Dog

Silly dog with rockstar glasses

Silly dog is obedient and does everything
Confident with people
Kind to friends
Yellow body and blue legs.

Rio Whittingham (8)
St Thomas Cantilupe CE Primary, Hereford

Rocky

R aces to get nuts
O nly listens to rock music
C hases rats
K ind and helpful
Y es, he's friendly.

Ted Waters (7)
St Thomas Cantilupe CE Primary, Hereford

Friendly Kraken

They have ears as blue as the sea
Brain as big as a dog
Mouths as tiny as a germ
Tongues as long as a fishing line.

Alejandro Roibu (7)
St Thomas Cantilupe CE Primary, Hereford

Pizza Pet

Spiky pepperoni eyes
Poisonous mushroom hands
Stinky blue cheese mouth
Four curly fry legs
Doughy body!

Tyson Harris
St Thomas Cantilupe CE Primary, Hereford

Friendly Kraken

Eyes as blue as the sky
Brain as smart as a smartypants
Mouth as tiny as a germ
Tongue as long as a tie.

Gina Tangjaritsakul (7)
St Thomas Cantilupe CE Primary, Hereford

Rocy

R ockstar shirt
O bedient to the lord
C heeky as a tiger
Y ellow as the sun.

Marcel Kozaczynski (8)
St Thomas Cantilupe CE Primary, Hereford

Geoff

Meet Geoff the Orca, he's my pet,
In the Atlantic Ocean is where we met,

Geoff is special because he can fly
A flying Orca, you might wonder why?

He flys to impress folks all over town
Flying around and around and around and around

Geoff is neon pink from his tale to his eyes
A neon pink Orca, you might wonder why?

He is pink so that he can always be found
Flying around and around and around and around

Geoff is the most amazing pet
I am always thankful for the day we met.

Abe Garner (8)
Stanford Junior School, Brighton

Peculiar Pet

The dog is a
Curled up ying yang on the
Carpet

She is a silhouette in the
Distance watching your
Path

She is like a sweet, melting
White chocolate on your
Tongue

Her tail wags like a humming
Bird's wing

She is my four-legged
Shadow

She is my superhero, saving
My day.

Mia Maclean (10)
Stanford Junior School, Brighton

Sunny The Smart Golden Dog

Sunny, the smartest dog ever on Earth,
He always saves me when I'm in a bad situation,
He is there at home,
We always play together,
He is my hero dog,
He's able to travel 300mph
Speed is his best thing,
Although, gets tired when running,
So loud on his walkie-talkie,
Never in trouble,
But always ready to help,
He always wins the dog races at his dog school,

He is the top dog in everything in the world,
He could even understand people,
He is one of my best buddies,
He is always there for me.

He is my hero,
And he will be my hero forever.

Emir Bayar (9)
The Literacy House International, Tintagel

Jumpy The Super Bunny

There lies Jumpy the super bunny
Waiting to start his journey,
The great old carrot advised him to do so,
For a week or so,
When he gets hungry he shall eat all of the tummies,
Belonging to the bunnies.

The journey begins in a tiny town,
Which is big and brown,
Made of soil and dirt
A comfy home perishes
Unfortunately, this was the home
Of Jumpy,
His life was taken and ruined
Not yet,
Jumpy had decided to begin his super life,
Billionaire already in his town,
A boss of his house, his wife, and all that lay around.

Built himself a secret lair,
With all the items a bunny could have,
Juicy carrots,
A loving human,
And a cosy cottage
Jumpy the bunny desired an advisor.
He knew the perfect man for the job,
Wisey, the great old carrot.
As advised he ate all those tummies,
Which made him stronger and faster,

Flying ability was next,
He asked his old old pal,
Jilly the cow,
To give him a hand to devise his super-powered plan,
Popping a bottle of limeade
To give him a boost,
Sliding into a supersuit,
Off he went into the sky,
Whoosh! He went off to his arch-enemies.

Hit the course Jumpy did,
With a kick, a bump and a skid,
So he plotted, Mow kick Pow,
Where Jilly named the first bad guy,
Pinky the Pig.

His end had been predicted,
Off he went,
His head went first,
His legs last.
This Pinky took it for all the piggies.
Jumpy soon gave up his super career,
Since his powers were waning and not of interest,
Oh, dear!
Jumpy the bunny's life returned to normal,
Awaiting a new career
What will it be?
Nobody knows!

Just wait and see!

Nolan Noronha (11)
The Literacy House International, Tintagel

Asia The Lady Dog

Living in a fancy mansion,
Here is the lady dog
Interested in fashion.
The best driver nowadays
She's driving her convertible on Mondays.
Her pink scarf is flying in waves,
Like a lady, she always behaves.
She invites the neighbour's dogs
For snacks and smart dialogues.
They particularly talk about politics
And who's the top dog in town
Lady President barks, *woof! Woof!*
Trying to convince the fat pigs
To join the Doggy Party
Promising to make them a smarty.
"Watch out, dear friends!"
Under the pinky scarf
There is a monster in disguise.
After all, she is just a fancy politician
Trying to keep her bone, as a large size.

But for me, she is the best dog of all
'Cause she is following her call.

Tahir Eralp Guzel (9)
The Literacy House International, Tintagel

Cuddler The Miniature Cat

Cuddler, the miniature cat,
Woke up and hopped out of bed.
Whispered, "Good morning," to his mother.
Yawed and... ACHOO!
Cuddler the miniature cat cuddled around
and for his breakfast drank milk.
He cuddled back around his mother, yawing.
I want to sleep.
Cuddler the miniature cat only 2 years old.
He strolled to his toys
He played
All day!
With his furry ball,
Wandering around.
Next, he went to his friend
Played catch the ball,
And pulled the string
The string was long and twisted
The ball was furry and sparkly,
Because his friend
Is a girl.

A girl cat that
He loved her dearly,
Oh yes he did!
But he didn't say so.
After that, he pounced
Back home.
More milk and a giant dog bone.
Cuddled around,
His mother once again.
He waddled,
To bed.
As he wasn't fed,
And went to sleep.
Without a PEEP!

Cuddler the miniature cat
He never grew fat
His body is always tiny.

He was my friend
My Cuddler.
My hero

My cat!

Layan Alachkar (8)
The Literacy House International, Tintagel

Cloud The Hamster Cuddler

The hamster wakes up,
Pounces straight out of bed.
He oils himself, from hip to head.

He goes to work on a big wheel of cheese.
Digging and digging on his way.
He finally pops at the bottom of the cheese,
In a big room of cheesy wheesy!

At one o'clock he puts on a cloak and scampers as fast as his tiny feet can carry him,
Faster and faster he goes,
He drops his bag,
Leaps on the couch and *creak*
the couch greets him.

The next day feels like a new dawn,
A card in the mailbox groaning in boredom.
"A birthday card?
Happy birthday to me!
I'm one year old!"

He jumps out of his little scrubby, dusty house,
Runs to Mum,
Returning a smile.
"Don't worry honey, I know how you feel."

My pet is a hamster that goes to work in a little jacket,
Goes to the gym with a little sack,
Makes a lot of a racket while stomping back home,
And loves to read before and after dawn!

He is my little hero,
Runs around like a little champion,
Love always shines around him like just like light,
My little hero he is.

Hani Alachkar (11)
The Literacy House International, Tintagel

My Hiding Hippopotamus

H iding in the long grass - a hippopotamus. But why is she in India?
I ndia is where she lives.
P robably she has been taken by animal control.
P eople might have taken her there so she can have a happy life.
O h yeah!
P robably her name is Perl.
O f course it is.
T omorrow her name is getting changed.
A gain.
M aybe her name is going to be...
U nna.
S uch a nice name!

Perla Nutu (8)
Ullapool Primary School, Ullapool

Pancatcakes

P eople get stung by him
A mazing at art
N o one bullies him
C lever as a penny
A dorable as the Queen of England
T exts on his syrupy phone
C ute as a bunny
A nnoying but cute!
K ind to his friend
E lectric like lightning
S limy as syrup.

Isabella Macdonald (8)
Ullapool Primary School, Ullapool

Elle

Splash, splash, she's big and tall.
She can grab things that are small and she can grab things that are tall.
Thump, thump, she eats a lot of grass.
She has big ears to hear the hunters shooting her family.
She's always upset unless her brother is there with her.

Lily Maclean (10)
Ullapool Primary School, Ullapool

The Dragon's Night

D angerous dragon.
R ed-hot flaming breath.
A wful dragon in the forest.
G ets everything it wants.
O n the hill and it lies sleeping, resting its head on a tree.
N ow's the time to get rid of the dragon, so they say.

Rhea Macleod (7)
Ullapool Primary School, Ullapool

Spider Cat

S assy and scaly
P retty hairy
I ncredibly strong
D angerous
E xtraordinary
"R oar!" he says at night

C lever
A dorable and has...
T iny feet!

Lily Walton (9)
Ullapool Primary School, Ullapool

Dark Matter Pet

He is purple
And his skin moves like a river.
His body is like a block,
He doesn't have any arms
And his eyes are round and white.
He likes to collect coins
And he sleeps upstairs.
He eats purple food.
He looks a bit evil
But I think he's nice.

Ewan Ross (8)
Ullapool Primary School, Ullapool

Snail

My snails are slimy.
Now they are munching on a treat.
Once a month - a strawberry.
Argh, I don't want my snails to get squished!
I walk around them carefully.
I want to make them a snail park.
Let's have dinner.

Scarlett Davis (8)
Ullapool Primary School, Ullapool

My Clever Pet

Poppy deer, your nose smells the grass.
It tastes like sweet, juicy water.
You are sensitive and like to be clean.
You run everywhere, no way to get you to stop.
I know you like me.

Chloe Hodgkinson (7)
Ullapool Primary School, Ullapool

Wonkywoozel

I have a pet Wonkywoozel.
I tie him on a lead.
He has sharp claws that could really make you bleed.
I like to feed him dog food, his favourite flavour, swede.

James Miller (9)
Ullapool Primary School, Ullapool

Juicy

I hear crunching on the leaves.
I smell a yummy body.
I feel the leg I'm slithering up.
I see the delicious face.
I taste the juicy blood of my owner.

Brodie Mackenzie (9)
Ullapool Primary School, Ullapool

Rabbit In The Hole

Hip hop into the dark streets.
First stop will be the scrap bin.
I'm looking for carrots for my feast.
Yeah! Hip hop back home.

Alisha Haughey (8)
Ullapool Primary School, Ullapool

Hunter

I am a dog
I am here for mice
I am hunting for mice
I have one
I am full of mice

I go back home
I hear the fire
I go to the fire

I go to sleep.

Lucas Mackay (9)
Ullapool Primary School, Ullapool

Frosty And Derpy Bacon

F rosty the flying magic dragon flies high in the sky.
R ising higher and higher with his friends.
O nly Frosty can freeze the ice cream.
S o cold is Frosty's ice breath, he can turn water into ice.
Y ummy ice cream is eaten by Frosty.

D erpy is Frosty's sidekick and friend.
E arl's chocolate ice cream is their favourite.
R unning fast they crashed into the wall. *Crash! Bang!*
"**P** hew!" they said. "Good job none of us got hurt!"
Y elling loudly, they heard the sirens so they began to attack the bad guy.

Best friends forever, they tried their best but couldn't succeed.

Joseph Powley (9)
Warwick Bridge Primary School, Warwick Bridge

Strong Steve

S trong Steve is stronger than the Hulk.
T he terrifying, ugly, six-eyed furry monster.
R aging monster has the eye of an eagle for food.
O n the door of his cave, is dead, rotting bones.
N ever give him a chance to be a dinner guest or you are the dinner!
G rowling in his cave that smells like dead meat, rotting away.

S teve is his name.
T errible, all the animals dead at his door.
E ven the smallest animal, from as small as a snail to as big as an elephant!
V ery hungry, he is always as hungry as a lion!
E normous is the size of his blood-dripping jaw of death.

Oliver Kelly (10)
Warwick Bridge Primary School, Warwick Bridge

Sid The Speedy Snail

S oaring through the city.
P ace as fast as the speed of light.
E asily setting trees on fire.
E ating all the food in the shops.
D azzling people with his incredible velocity.
Y ellow sun reflecting off his vibrant shell.

S nails are in awe of his amazing pace.
N ever challenge Sid to a race.
A s dangerous as a nuke about to explode.
I would evacuate the area when Sid is around.
L ike a bullet Sid zoomed off and set another building on fire.

Noah Samuel Fielden (9)
Warwick Bridge Primary School, Warwick Bridge

Berry And Barry The Bedtime Sheep

B aa! Baa! went Barry as he was strolling on the narrow street.

A s he was prancing on the street, he found a silent field just as the sun was rising.

R oaming as the morning sun was rising on the dark streets, Barry found a fantastic farmer who decided to raise him.

R aising him was back-breakingly hard, so he found a friend called Berry. She was sweet so the farmer decided to put them together forever.

Y awning as the moon rose, Berry and Barry the bedtime sheep fell fast asleep.

Harry James Richardson (8)
Warwick Bridge Primary School, Warwick Bridge

Crystal The Ice Dragon

Bash! Crash!
Crystal arose from a deep slumber.
A number of rocks flung off her as she stood proudly.
Zing! Zing!
The sound of her huge nails scraping against the rocks, numbing the brains of people.
Her shimmering scales shine smartly in the sparkling sun.
Glistening teeth covered in a silvery, slimy substance.
Blue eyes as cold as the Arctic.
Roar! Roar! Roar!
Crystal threw her mighty head back angrily at the sight of the sun.
Would you want this pet?

Elena Lily Archibald (9)
Warwick Bridge Primary School, Warwick Bridge

Silly Scout

S cout runs madly with his big pink tongue hanging out.
I n the garden, he chews his toys.
L ovely dog with fur as soft as a teddy bear.
L ike a torpedo, he is very fast.
Y ummy steak is his favourite food.

S cout loves to chase pheasants in the wood.
C hasing deer is his favourite thing.
O n a walk, he gets excited.
U nder the blanket, you hear him snoring.
T aking him for a walk is a challenge.

Eliza Forster (9)
Warwick Bridge Primary School, Warwick Bridge

Steve The Sock Scavenger

S tomp! goes Steve's unbreakable foot as it rapidly plummets to the ground.
T im the bouncing Tigger is then squashed by Steve's colossal foot (RIP).
E very person on Earth is trembling with fear and worried that they are too going to get squashed.
V anessa the news reporter is stomped on on live television.
E ven Terry the Tortoise (famous rugby player) is terrified of Steve the Sock Scavenger.

Charlie Broatch (9)
Warwick Bridge Primary School, Warwick Bridge

Candy The Candy Dog

C andy was sick with sugar and sweets like a water pipe exploding with pressure.

A man walks up and crunch, he picks up some sweets and runs away.

N ever eat Candy's sweets.

D an the man is walking home eating all the sweets. *Boom!* goes Dan and he is never to be seen again.

Y ikes goes Candy and she runs away, as frightened as a zebra that is being chased by a lion.

Colin Abbott (9)
Warwick Bridge Primary School, Warwick Bridge

Super Doggy

S uper Doggy can fly like a lightning bolt flying in the air.

"**U** nmask now," said one of the people, "to see if you are the real Super Doggy."

"**P** lease can you unmask now? You look like a lion!" said one of the people.

E xciting, *boom!* There was a boom and Super Doggy saved the people.

R andomly, he zoomed around the capital of the country.

Oliver Horne (9)
Warwick Bridge Primary School, Warwick Bridge

Rolo And Romeo The Talented Rabbits

Rolo is as fluffy as a silky teddy bear.
Romeo is as funny as a joke.
Rolo and Romeo rushed roughly in a solid brown bridge.
Zoom! Rolo quickly jumped in the air.
Bang! Romeo thumped on the wooden ground.
Rolo and Romeo ran right through a brown branch.
Rolo and Romeo are very talented.
Splash! Rolo and Romeo jumped in the freezing water.

Olivia Brown (9)
Warwick Bridge Primary School, Warwick Bridge

Therry The Swiper

Therry the swiper has giant claws which he uses for swiping lots of danger.
At night, Therry slowly walks around the tiny neighbourhood.
Scanning for fresh, yummy trees to eat using his neck that is as long as a snake.
While he walks, his scary, stomping, swiping claws are swinging from side to side.
Rooaarrrr!
Therry finally scares away an adult T-rex.

Will James Mackie (8)
Warwick Bridge Primary School, Warwick Bridge

Nessie

N essie plays during the black night.
E veryone is asleep, nobody notices her.
S ome people say that Nessie is terribly terrifying.
S ome say Nessie is a cuddly, cute monster.
I think Nessie eats slimy, sloppy fish.
E agerly, Nessie dives down into the deep dark water.

Splash!

Georgia Fricker (8)
Warwick Bridge Primary School, Warwick Bridge

Star The Sparkling Starfish

Star is even more glittery than a big pot of glitter.
Sparkling star, shining like a crystal.
Star the starfish is as sparkly as the sun.
Bam! goes some of her glitter into the air.
Star is very helpful and kind and secretly a superhero!
Click, click, click, as she moves on the crazy-looking rock.

Ava-Mae Wilson-Marks (9)
Warwick Bridge Primary School, Warwick Bridge

Happy The Hilarious Horse

H appy the beautiful brown horse went neigh! Neigh! very loudly.
A s happy as children when they get a death-by-chocolate ice cream.
P rancing gracefully through the green grassy field.
P acing through the field looking for juicy apples.
Y outhful and joyfully, Happy plays all day.

Jasmine Loader (8)
Warwick Bridge Primary School, Warwick Bridge

Molly The Unicycle And Tightrope Giraffe

M olly the big and beautiful giraffe.
O n the tightrope, her elegant head reaches the roof like a tower.
L ikely going to fall. Argh!
L ovely Molly is a spotty and long-necked giraffe who is as good as a gymnast.
Y ou could be as good as her one day.

Elsa Watson (8)
Warwick Bridge Primary School, Warwick Bridge

Jumpy Jeb The Dog Giraffe

Jumpy Jeb was as huge as a 10-foot tall house. He was also strange like Matt the big, icky rat. Jeb's self-confidence was as small as an ant. Jeb's birthdays were as silent and lonely as the woods at night.
Tap, tap, tap went the sound of Jeb's bony legs.

Dylan Mackay (10)
Warwick Bridge Primary School, Warwick Bridge

Slowpoke

S o slow
L ies in bed all day
O ld and grumpy
W alks so slow
P atrolling its trees
O h they are so lazy
K ing of the trees
E ats so much.

Finlay James Kerr (7)
West Primary School, Paisley

Monkey

M y monkey is always hungry
O h they are funny!
N othing else is funny
K ing of the trees
E veryone likes him
Y ellow funny monkey.

Logan Deery Bruce
West Primary School, Paisley

Flash

F lying through the sky
L ike a fast rocket
A very fast speedy dog
S hooting through the stars
H igh as a cloud.

Sarah Garrett (7)
West Primary School, Paisley

Bruce

B ruce is my funny dog.
R eally cute.
U nique dancer.
C uddly and caring.
E xtremely energetic.

Abyaan Memon (8)
West Primary School, Paisley

A Miniature Magic Talking Rabbit

He always makes me happy,
This little pet of mine,
I keep him in his bed,
Or hold him in my arms,
I take him with me to school,
And the teacher doesn't realise,
He talks right through art,
It's me that gets told off!
At home, he's locked away
A cage that glows at night,
We like to play with toys,
And when Nan's not looking,
He climbs the back fence,
Searching for snacks.

Imogen Turner (8)
Westminster Community Primary School, Ellesmere Port

My Pet Carrot

My pet is a carrot
A carrot is my pet
It is my friend
My very best friend
We do everything together
I never want to leave it
Although it's turning brown
And my pocket is all smushy
I love my friend the carrot.

Sean Machell (7)
Westminster Community Primary School, Ellesmere Port

My Two-Headed Snake

I keep her in my wardrobe,
I check her once a minute,
She's often on my shoulder,
Or beneath my jumper,
She loves Mum's milk,
But Mum doesn't know,
Neither does anyone else.

Summer Forde (7)
Westminster Community Primary School, Ellesmere Port

My Pet Watch - Visible Only To Me

I keep him on my wrist,
Only I can see him,
We chat every hour,
He dings and ticks,
To tell me secrets,
I tell him mine back.

Jayden Cato (7)
Westminster Community Primary School, Ellesmere Port

Young Writers Information

We hope you have enjoyed reading this book – and that you will continue to in the coming years.

If you're a young writer who enjoys reading and creative writing, or the parent of an enthusiastic poet or story writer, do visit our website www.youngwriters.co.uk. Here you will find free competitions, workshops and games, as well as recommended reads, a poetry glossary and our blog. There's lots to keep budding writers motivated to write!

If you would like to order further copies of this book, or any of our other titles, then please give us a call or order via your online account.

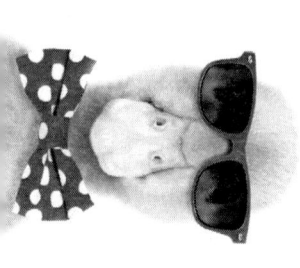

Young Writers
Remus House
Coltsfoot Drive
Peterborough
PE2 9BF
(01733) 890066
info@youngwriters.co.uk

Join in the conversation!
Tips, news, giveaways and much more!

YoungWritersUK @YoungWritersCW